RIGHT WOMAN, WRONG MAN. RIGHT MAN, WRONG WOMAN.

ZOEHANN DENNIS

Right Woman, Wrong man. Right Man, Wrong Woman.

This book is written to provide information and motivation to readers. Its purpose is not to render any type of psychological, legal, or professional advice of any kind. The content is the sole opinion and expression of the author, and not necessarily that of the publisher.

Copyright © 2021 by Zoehann Dennis.

All rights reserved. No part of this book may be reproduced, transmitted, or distributed in any form by any means, including, but not limited to, recording, photocopying, or taking screenshots of parts of the book, without prior written permission from the author or the publisher. Brief quotations for noncommercial purposes, such as book reviews, permitted by Fair Use of the U.S. Copyright Law, are allowed without written permissions, as long as such quotations do not cause damage to the book's commercial value. For permissions, write to the publisher, whose address is stated below.

Printed in the United States of America.

ISBN 978-1-955363-22-8 (Paperback)
ISBN 978-1-955363-23-5 (Digital)

Lettra Press books may be ordered through booksellers or by contacting:

Lettra Press LLC
30 N Gould St. Suite 4753
Sheridan, WY 82801
1 307-200-3414 | info@lettrapress.com
www.lettrapress.com

This book is dedicated to

The persons suffering in silence, traumatized and held hostage by fear. The people who were misguided and manipulated into making a commitment they have now lived to regret. To the survivors of domestic violence and their children.

God loves you and someone is praying for you.

To the person that spoke up for the one being abused and bullied. To the person that prayed and obeyed the voice of God to rescue the hurting.

You are an answered prayer! Thank you.

TABLE OF CONTENTS

Acknowledgment vii
Preface ix
Chapter 1   Love 1
Chapter 2   Christian and Single 8
Chapter 3   Am I Unequally Yoked? 14
Chapter 4   Right Woman 20
Chapter 5   Wrong Man 24
Chapter 6   Right Man 30
Chapter 7   Wrong Woman 35
Chapter 8   Marriage Hoax 45
Chapter 9   Your Children 50
Chapter 10   Wicked Affections 53
Chapter 11   Domestic Violence 56
Chapter 12   Submit to Love 59
Chapter 13   Are you in Agreement? 63
Chapter 14   Love Yourself 71
Chapter 15   Start over strong 79

ACKNOWLEDGMENT

To the one True God; the King of all Kings; my strength; my Rock; a Friend that is closer than a brother; the restorer of my soul-Jesus Christ my Lord!

This book is a long time coming, though it's small and very few pages, it was no easy undertaking. I wrote it through the grace and strength of God.

All glory to the True and Living, Most High God, "For in Him we live and move and have our being;" *Acts 17:28 KJV.*

I hope this book will help to deliver someone in bondage or prevent someone from entering a situation of spiritual bondage.

To my family, I love you and thank you for the continued support.

To my dear close friends and everyone who continually supports my ministry, I love and appreciate you, thank you!

PREFACE

We all share in the universal need to be loved.

Since we are created in the image of God, we are created in love. The ultimate purpose of this love is to please God.

But we have lost the essence of what love truly means. Society has bombarded our minds with endless distractions caused by financial strain, compromise, immorality, ungodly lifestyles and relationships based on personal gratification without commitment. I am here to remind you that love is the very essence of who God is, his love is selfless and sacrificial, it protects at all costs and is fully established in righteousness.

God's love for us has proven time and time again, that whether we feel His presence or not; whether we have broken His words or not; His Love remains the same. David asked in *Psalm 139:7, "Whither shall I go from your Spirit? or whither shall I flee from your presence?"* David understood the depths of God's love.

Loving someone is evident in what you do, whether in their presence or their absence.

I advise you to wait on true love. It will be worth the wait.

The Bible gives us the description of what true love is.

"Love is patient, love is kind. It does not envy, it does not boast, it is not proud. **It does not dishonor others, it** *is not self-seeking, it is not easily angered,* <u>*it keeps no record of wrongs*</u>*. Love does not delight in evil but rejoices with the truth. It always protects, always trusts, always hopes, always perseveres." 1 Corinthians 13:4-7 (NIV)*

BE CAREFUL.

Be careful who you give your heart to. Be careful who you let into your life, because some persons enter your life to trap you and only God can deliver you from these situations.

I personally know individuals who were held captive by obsessive, selfish, evil partners that were psychologically manipulative. In some instances, witchcraft was used to spiritually manipulate with devised plots that led to their untimely death.

Give your **HEART** to God. Love Him. Trust **ONLY** in Him.

"Rest in the Lord and **wait patiently** *for Him." (Psalm 37:7) KJV.*

Remember whatever God does, he does to complete perfection.

The Bible reminds us:

- When God chose a king, he chose one after His own heart. David was God's choice.

- When God chose a deliverer for Israel from Pharaoh, he chose a meek one. God's choice was Moses.

- When God chose a warrior, he chose a bold one. God chose Joshua.

- When God wanted a people to call His is own, He chose Father Abraham, a man of great Faith.

There are numerous scriptures listing the <u>chosen</u> throughout the Bible. Let these scriptures remind you that God's choices were by an individual's **heart**- who they truly are.

Let God choose for you, have faith in God and be patient. We are uniquely created. Our individualities can deter others, because some of us are not always easy to deal with and that is why, we must wait on God while He prepares your future spouse. God is makings sure both of you are compatible for each other before He connects you to that special person.

CHAPTER 1

Love

A deep connection and strong affection demonstrated by choosing to **give** selflessly, sacrificially and unconditionally.

The Love that capsules all types of love, is the Agape love; this is the one that stands the test of time. Love for all mankind is selfless.

Types of love examined in this chapter are:

Eros – sexual or passionate love.

Philia – friendship love, trust and companionship

Storge – familial love between children and parents, born out of fondness, dependability and familiarity.

When we examine these three types of love, the recurring theme is the act of giving.

Dictionary.com defines the word Giving as, "to present voluntarily and without expecting compensation ……"

Love is not demonstrated only by giving material or tangible things. It is possible to feel loved by someone without the exchange of tangible gifts. Conversely, you could be showered with gifts and not feel loved because you don't have that individual's time or heart.

When God **gave** His son Jesus Christ as a sacrificial lamb, God, who is a Spirit, entered the world in human form and through Christ, He gave Himself.

Philippians 2: 6KJV *"Let this mind be in you, which was also in Christ Jesus: Who, being in the form of God, thought it not robbery to be equal with God: But made himself of no reputation, and took upon him the form of a **servant** and was made in the likeness of men: And being found in fashion as a man, **he humbled himself**, and became obedient unto death, even of the cross."*

The mechanics of giving includes taking from one source to provide for another. There should be a sense of fulfilment and accomplishment when you give genuinely. When you have given your best, there is no feeling of regret. Giving satisfies. It creates joy and promotes a spirit of gratitude and love for others

Acts 20:35 KJV reminds us, "…*it is more **blessed to give** than to receive*".

God loves a cheerful giver. His word declares *"Give and it shall be given unto you, good measure, pressed down and shaken together and running over, shall men give into your bosom. For with the same measure that ye mete withal it shall be measured to you again"* Luke **6:38** KJV.

The way we give, is the way we receive. If we give cheerfully and with a clean heart, expecting nothing in return, then God will pour deserved blessings into our lives.

There are individuals who struggle with giving, or who gives sparingly. Many persons are miserable and constantly worrying about their possessions, fearful of losing even the smallest thing. This presence of fear reveals the absence of love.

Is it greed? This unquenchable need for more, no matter the quest, simply means nothing can truly bring satisfaction. Whether it is greed or fear, the scripture provides recourse, *see "There is no fear in love; but perfect love casteth out fear: because fear hath torment. He that feareth is not made perfect in love." 1 John 4:18* KJV

*"For God hath **not** given us the **spirit** of fear but of POWER and **of LOVE** and of a SOUND MIND" 2 Timothy 1:7KJV*

Be mindful that life is a cycle and what goes around, comes around.

The scripture says, *"Be not deceived; God is not mocked: for whatsoever a man soweth that shall he also reap" Galatians 6 :7* KJV.

God observes our actions, if we hold back in giving, then our expectations in receiving should be measured by our own acts of giving.

How liberating it is to give, to release something of value to another in need without expecting anything in return. My friends, that is the **Spirit of Love in manifestation.**

It would be nice if your generosity is always appreciated, but sometimes it's not and that's okay. A genuine giver gives happily, whether it's unappreciated or appreciated. Their motivation to give, isn't impacted by the receiver's ungratefulness or lack of recognition. Don't be sadden by others inability to receive your help or gift of love, some people refuse external help from others even if it is beneficial to them.

When an individual is struggling with substance abuse issues and refuses counseling or an intervention from close friends and family members; it is discouraging and disappointing because it leads to feelings of hopelessness. It is the love we have for the one suffering that pushes us to save them by any means necessary. You would **give** anything to save them!

This is what God did for us. He saw a world drowning in sin, the desolation required more than the usual sacrifices of bulls and goats to cancel the judgment of eternal death, which is the result of sinfulness. God gave his only Son, because that was the only way to redeem mankind. He willingly gave His only Son Jesus Christ.

"For God so loved the world, that he **gave** his **ONLY** begotten son that whosoever believeth in him should not perish but have everlasting life". **John 3:16KJV**

I know this is a very popular scripture that needs little or no interpretation. But for so many it has become a cliché, but can we just take a minute to think about this?

- God the omnipresent (always everywhere)
- God the omniscient (knowing everything)

God the Creator of all things. Yes! This God created you and I, for His purpose and in His image. He gave us free will to choose, to worship Him, to serve him faithfully but humanity chose to abandon Him and worship the worldly possessions that sprung from His creation.

Imagine this scenario:

As a mother, you carry your baby for nine months. You hand selected all the clothes and newborn items you'll need to ensure the baby is healthy and strong, you changed your diet and eliminate toxic habits that are harmful to your precious child. You anticipate the journey of motherhood, the places and people you'll visit and most importantly which of your favorite features your child will inherit. Even after the horrors of childbirth, you find love and happiness in the face of the long-awaited blessing- your baby.

As your child grows, you encounter a situation in which the child clings to or embraces a stranger or family member and refuses to detach and return to your arms. You find yourself wondering, how do I get my child to want me and cling to me and **love me?**

In a similar way God is longing to receive love from his children, love with our whole hearts. How do we love Him? A simple act of giving- by **giving** our lives to Him. By **giving** our best and our worst to Him. When you truly love someone, you **give** them your heart, right? God wants it all.

When two people are in-love, they give their all to each other. There is no separation, what's yours is mine and vice versa. We *give* our all to each other. We become one, a part of each other with no intention to abuse or hurt each other. The Bible tells us in **Romans 13:10KJV** that *"Love worketh no ill to his neighbor, therefore love is the fulfilling of the law."*

When two people fall in love with each other, love is shown by a **continuous cycle of giving**.

Love in action is:
Giving your time
Giving help when needed
Giving support
Giving care
Giving sacrificially
Giving pleasure
Giving honesty (gently)
Give selflessly
Giving respect
Giving your best

God is a Spirit, and He is the manifestation of love. Since we are created in His image, we are capable of loving, that is *giving* of oneself unconditionally because we are made from love.

Therefore, the Spirit of God is intertwined in all our being to **give** ourselves selflessly and unconditionally to someone worthy of it, but God should be the **first** recipient. God created the institution of marriage for the demonstration of love between a man and woman, for a marriage to be based on love it must be God-centered and the union must be <u>divinely joined and ordained</u> by God.

*"But from the beginning of the creation God made them male and female. For this cause shall man leave his father and mother and cleave to his wife; And they twain shall be one flesh: so, then they are no more twain, but one flesh. <u>What therefore **God hath joined together**</u>, let not man put asunder."* ***Mark 10:6 – 9***KJV

Friends, who God has <u>united</u> together <u>in the spirit of His love</u>, nothing or no one can separate, because whatever God does, is well done and orchestrated.

Be aware, that the sin of unforgiveness can enter a God ordained union and cause separation. Nonetheless, reconciliation is possible if partners learn to forgive and continue to pursue God's divine will for their lives together. This is specific to persons that God divinely joined together. There are marriages that should never have happened and even with forgiveness it will never work because the union is against God's divine will, it hinders you from fulfilling your God assigned purpose and does not bring God any glory. **Read: Ezra Chapter 10**

Forgiveness is an act of **giving**, a demonstration of love.

It is giving up your bitterness, **giving** up your choice to be angry, **giving** in to pardon, grace and mercy. The **giving** of a second chance. It is God's forgiveness of our sins through the shed blood of Jesus Christ that has reconciled us to Him.

Colossians 1:19-20 KJV tells us; "For it pleased the Father that in him should all fulness dwell; And, having made peace through the blood of his cross, by him to reconcile all things unto himself…"

REMEMBER TO LOVE YOURSELF TOO.

CHAPTER 2

Christian and Single

Being a single born-again Christian is fantastic! If you are on fire to work for God and certain of your calling and purpose, that's awesome! But how do you handle loneliness and abstinence? When your only company is the Holy Spirit, yes, His Spirit.

God satisfies my soul and my spirit but my body? Where is my companion, friend, helpmate, my rib match, my wife, my husband, my soul mate, God's choice for me?

Friends, this is a reality, and it gets hard sometimes. We all have needs, a need for: physical contact, to be heard, to have someone actively listen to you, to have complete command of their attention, a hug, for someone to ask, "How are you? How is your day going? … need for companionship and yes, a need to be sexually satisfied.

In these moments. The voice of the Lord makes a difference. He says: "be patient, be humble and **wait**". We may ask God, "Haven't I waited? I've been single for so long. His response, "the BEST is worth waiting for". A response like that gives you hope that a future spouse does exists. The spouse God has created and crafted for each of us comes in God's timing.

When you've surrendered your all to God, the enemy sends numerous distractions to mislead you, but keep your focus on Christ the Solid Rock.

"…<u>seek</u> ye <u>first</u> the kingdom of God and his righteousness … all these things shall be added unto you" ***Matthew 6: 33.KJV***

This is NOT just an old saying …<u>it's the word of God, a divine instruction.</u>

There will be times when you're single and you'll feel out-of-touch, forgotten or even abandoned. Everyone around you is dating or courting or getting engaged but what about me? You may ask.

There is a reason you are alone right now. God is preparing your spouse, the right person; the chosen; the ordained one. God is trimming, grooming and molding them to be compatible with you. He is working on you as well, being single is a part of your preparation. A woman is not born a wife nor a man a husband. Some persons don't even have the desire to be a spouse.

A Christian woman once told me, the purpose of marriage is for sexual satisfaction and procreation, and she has no interest in being a wife. If she has the gift to stay celibate like Paul in 1Corinthians 7:7-8 KJV then she'll be ok.

A ministry is a work or vocation. **Marriage is a ministry**; marriage isn't just a sanctuary for sex.

A minister attends to someone's needs. Marriage is about <u>giving</u> and sharing selflessly, attending to the needs of your spouse holistically, working as a team to achieve God's divine purpose together.

You cannot commit to the same activities and lifestyle habits you had being single, in your marriage. This can strain your marriage, and you might not have the capacity to balance both. Your interest will be divided.

"the <u>unmarried woman careth for the</u> <u>things of the Lord, that she may be holy in body and in spirit</u>: but she that is married careth for the things of the world, how she may please her husband." **1Corinthians 7:34KJV**

Dear ladies, don't rush to marry just any Christian guy that comes with a ring and men don't be deceived by the wolves in sheep's clothing batting her eyelashes. Don't be deceived by loneliness, or empty promises or a religious leader pressuring you to marry when you're not ready. Don't be pressured into marriage because of your age or your friends or your family.

<u>**WAIT**</u> !!, Wait on the Lord, I know of long marriages that didn't last, after 31yrs, 17yrs, 4yrs, 13yrs, 2yrs, 10yrs, 6yrs, 25yrs that have failed, oops ... correction, NO!! they did not fail, <u>they **were NOT ordained by God,**</u> it was in His permissive will**,** that's how you got married to that person, He simply allowed it outside of His divine will, because it is what you chose to do with your free will.

When your marriage is not ordained or joined by God, you will **never** become one and God has the authority to separate that union to eventually bring you into His divine will.

Ladies, Stop! Do not chase men, please. That is not the order of God. That's a man's job, it's in his nature to pursue you. Seek you out, let him express his interest and intentions in a respectful manner. Even if God reveals your husband, you'll still have to wait to be united in God's timing.

Ephesians 5:31 "For this cause shall **a man leave his father and mother and shall be joined unto his wife** and the two shall be one flesh."

It is the man that leaves his family to be with his wife. Let's look how God brought Isaac and Rebekah together.

This was Abraham's servant's prayer of petition, asking the Lord to <u>show him Isaac's wife.</u>

"Oh Lord, God of my master Abraham, I pray thee send me good speed this day, and show kindness unto my master Abraham. Behold I stand here by the well of water and the daughters of the men of the city come out to draw water. And let it come to pass, that the damsel to whom I shall say let down thy pitcher, I pray thee that I may drink, and she shall say, drink and I will give thy camels drink also: let the same be she that thou hast **appointed** for thy servant Isaac; and thereby shall I know that thou hast shewed kindness unto my master". ***Genesis 24 vs 12.***

Abraham sent his servant to find a wife for his son according to God's will. She was sought and found. The Lord is watching your attitude towards men.

Genesis 24 vs 21 says, "And the man wondering at her held his peace."

In silence he watched her, she was very kind and humble to him and his camels, the Lord showed him exactly what he asked to see - humility, kindness, tenderness, consideration and patience.

The question is, are you ready to be a wife? Not to have a wedding or have lots of sex and have babies. Marriage isn't an opportunity to display your wedding ring, house, children or husband.

What motivates your desire for marriage? Is it centered around your passion to be a good wife? Being a helpmate and having a family? What kind of woman are you? Are you controlling? Brawling? Or a manipulative Jezebel underneath that fancy dress and makeup?

Let's be real, can we be real? After you've made love, you would like to have food in the house, right? You must contribute to your marriage, not just your body. Do you help with laundry? or help pay bills, do you have your own income?

When living a married life there are responsibilities that are going to be established between both of you and it's important for you to play your part. You're not a roommate with benefits, it's a life partnership.

Take your time, allow God to prepare you for the wife role while He prepares the man for his husband role as well. So you will be prepared for his son, the man God is molding for you.

Be alert and sensitive in the spirit so that you'll be able to discern the anxiety attacks from the enemy- the sense of loneliness that overwhelms and tempts you to yield to Mr. or Mrs. Wrong. My brothers, are you ready to be a husband? Are you a good listener? Good communicator? are you sensitive?

Being a husband is a responsibility, you are responsible for being the priest or leader in your home. Most women are very expressive and partially communicate with body language, do you communicate well? are you ready to learn her unique body expressions? Are you patient enough to connect with her soul to meet her most essential needs? Are you able to express your emotions? Women need men to mean what they say, to be a man of their words and show it in their actions. Have a solid job or source of income, be responsible and reliable but we also want to connect, we want to be in sync.

We desire a bond built on love and respect. Ask God to create within you the uniqueness specifically required for the wife He has chosen for you.

GOD IS NEVER IN A RUSH!

CHAPTER 3

Am I Unequally Yoked?

God created us to procreate. Our bodies are made to reproduce. God gave us the desire, the urge and passion to mate, so the desire for intimacy is natural.

The institution of marriage allows a <u>man</u> and a <u>woman</u> to come together.

"And the Lord God said, it is not good for man to be alone…" (**Genesis 2:18**)

Is this person my equal? What makes him or her my equal? Is it because you attend the same church and we're both Christians? No.

God looks at a man's heart. If you find yourself interested in someone, you should seek the Lord about that person's heart, so that God can reveal their heart's true intentions. When Samuel the prophet was sent by God to anoint one of the sons of Jesse to be the next King of Israel, the prophet saw Eliab and was convinced he was the anointed one just by looking at him, but God rejected him.

"But the LORD said to Samuel, look not at his countenance or on the height of his stature, because I have refused him: for God sees not as man seeth: for man looketh on the outward appearance but the Lord looketh at the heart. **1 Samuel 16:7** KJV

If God reveals that person's heart is evil and yours is pure, you are unequally yoked.

If you are a born-again Christian married to a witch or wizard or someone practicing witchcraft or the dark arts, then you are unequally yoked.

If you are married to a person that doesn't believe Jesus Christ is God manifested in the flesh and opposes your faithfulness to God, then you are unequally yoked.

If you are in a relationship or married and your spouse continuously abuses you physically, verbally, emotionally, mentally and violate your human rights (treats you like an animal) then you are unequally yoked.

Some people have sex for different reasons. I asked different persons what is sex for them? These are some of their answers.

"It's a stress reliever, to reproduce, it's a need, convenience, a pass time, to get and give pleasure…"

What's important, is who do you desire sex from?

Think about it, what's the real purpose for making love? I would say to give pleasure, to express your love and to **become one** with the partner God has given you and reproduce.

The Bible defines making love as - to know or knew.

Genesis 4:1 "And Adam *knew* Eve his wife; and she conceived …"

To know, in the Hebrew language means: Yada, it's versatile and the definition changes across context. In the Bible's context, it's an intimate kind of knowledge, in complete detail; to study, analyze or investigate someone or something completely.

Yada - is dedicating ourselves to a person we will engage with love and affection completely.

Sex within a marriage is the safest, because it is with your one faithful partner. Sex outside a committed marriage is not safe! Wearing a condom is not 100 % safe either, you're at risk of contracting an STD or unwanted pregnancy or worst, a demonic transference or manipulation, dishonoring and sinning against your body, defiling what is the temple of the Holy Spirit of God.

Engaging in sexual intercourse automatically connects you to a person's spirit, whether you have chemistry or not their spirit lingers with you even after they're physically gone. But you've already formed a soul tie with this person which can hold on to you in their heart and soul and vice versa. Only Jesus Christ can break that bond, any strings attached must be detached in the name of Jesus Christ!

1 Corinthians 6:15 – 17 reminds us, "Know ye not that your bodies are the members of Christ? Shall I then take the members of Christ, and make them the members of a harlot? God forbid.…. What? know ye not that he is joined to a harlot is one body? For two, saith he, shall be one flesh… But he that is joined unto the Lord is one spirit".

If you are joined to an ungodly person, a part of your spirit has connected with their spirit as well. Ask the Lord to break all ties and spiritual bonds that is still intact. Ask the Lord to disconnect your spirit from the ungodly.

2 Corinthians 6:14 – 15 states.

"Be ye not unequally yoked together: with unbelievers for what fellowship hath righteousness with unrighteousness? And what communion hath light with darkness? And what concord hath Christ with Belial? …".

It's Satan's plan to connect us with individuals who are heading in the opposite direction. He lures you in with false attractions and false desires; blinds us with false hope, manipulation and fantasy. Satan traps us in the wrong relationships; a false and unequal one. This unequal union orchestrated by satan, sets the stage for a life of continuous lack and discontentment, desiring more from your partner but more is something that they cannot give because you're not equal- you're incompatible.

Then satan tricks you into believing you have to stay; he convinces you to commit. But you cannot commit to a false union, but you feel trapped to stay because of the children, tradition, image or culture- especially because of what people are going to think and say about you. So, you continue living a lie but remember you're only lying to yourself.

Be reminded, you're purpose in life is not to please people. <u>You were created to please</u> <u>God</u>. Is God pleased with the life you're living now? Is your current relationship pleasing God? Is He the foundation of the relationship? Does God hold first place in your life? Does your relationship reflect Christ's <u>love</u> for the church? Remember, the <u>church</u> is the bride of Christ, submitting <u>herself</u> to Jesus Christ her groom. ***Ephesians 5:22 – 33.***

What have you learned during your waiting period? After all these years, what are you offering? What have your experience taught you? The entire world works on a system of give and take. After you've received an education, you give back to society by using the knowledge you've gained and your given money for it.

What do you have to give your husband? What do you have to give your wife? This isn't only about material things. Are you emotionally stable and mentally healthy?

Are you spiritually grounded in Jesus Christ? Have you disconnected yourself fully from past intimate relationships? Have you gotten rid of pictures, gifts, keepsakes, feelings, the hurt, the regrets? Are you still wrestling with unresolved issues and the memories? These questions must be addressed and resolved before moving forward or there's trouble ahead. Don't bring emotions from the past into a new relationship with someone else.

Are you ready to **give** all of you? To **get** all of him or her **equally**?

When you are connected with your equal, you are in an equally yoked marriage. You'll both be on the same page; going in the same direction and with compatible goals. You will be able to communicate with glances and expressions, without words. An equally yoked marriage is in sync. You'll feel like you've known each other for years. Your equal will reflect you naturally, almost another you, but of course with differences.

Disagreements will be resolved with peaceful conversations, at times arguments may get intense but forgiveness is always on standby.

DO NOT ENTERTAIN CONFUSION.

CHAPTER 4

Right Woman

Men are seeking a woman to love, one that is soft, gentle, respectful and yes! A submissive woman, not someone to push around and instruct what to do, but to respect his leadership.

1 Peter 3:4 – 6 KJV "But let it be the hidden man of the heart, in that which is not corruptible, the ornament of a **meek** and **quiet spirit**, which is in the **sight of God** of **great price**. For after this manner in the old time the holy women also, who trusted in God, adorned themselves, being in subjection unto their own husbands:"……. Even as Sara obeyed Abraham, calling him lord: whose daughters ye are, as long as ye do well, and are not afraid with any amazement"

"Likewise, ye husbands, dwell with them according to knowledge, giving honor unto the wife, as unto the weaker vessel, and as being heirs together of the grace of life; that your prayers be not hindered" **1 Peter 3:7** KJV

Men, God will lead you to the right woman or the right woman will be presented to you. He will set up the meet, as you cross paths or as in the case of Abraham's servant, have someone bring her to you if there was no chance of you being where she is.

The woman God has appointed to you will be all that you need and even exceed your expectations; she will be a blessing to your life.

Genesis 24:14 KJV "And let it come to pass, that the damsel to whom I shall say, let down thy pitcher, I pray thee, that I may drink; and she shall say, Drink, and I will give thy camels drink also: let the same be she that thou hast **appointed** for thy servant Isaac; and thereby shall I know that thou hast showed kindness unto my master". Rebekah was that woman. She was kind, patient and thoughtful. When God is choosing your life partner, he is watching you, testing you, how do you treat men, how do you treat strangers, are you HELPFUL? How can you be a help meet if you don't like to help, offer assistance, or contribute to teamwork?

Ladies the next stranger you meet could be your husband or the person that connects you to him.

Some of the main characteristics of a wife is being understanding, patient, respectful, helpful, dependable, responsible and much more. She doesn't want her husband to do it all. She wants to share the responsibilities in achieving their goals.

The right woman will make you happy 95% of the time, the other 5% is just what makes you and her different which can be challenging but learn her ways and work around it, at times her emotions may be a little more in excess but that's when she needs to be held close, but some women won't say it.

With the right woman you will be complete. You will wait for her with pleasure because you know she will be worth it. As you take the time to know her, your love for her will increase and so will your respect for her. She will be the **only one** you desire in every way, and all your future plans will include her.

She will respect you and honor all your request to the best of her ability in the Lord ofcourse. She will represent you well in your absence, you will be proud of her. Becoming one won't take long or be a struggle because you both will desire most of the same things, goals, dreams and ideas. The right woman's genuine submission to her husband, will arouse him and in return he can't help but express his love and appreciation for the gift of a good wife that God has blessed him with.

A quote from my Dad "No woman runs from love". No woman that a man treats well is going to leave him, not a good woman that is. I'm not talking about wicked women that wants to stay in a man's life to use him for his money/security and whatever else they can get with their own selfish agendas. I'm speaking of genuine faithful, God fearing women that are committed to God first.

"Whoso findeth a wife findeth a good thing and <u>obtaineth favor of the Lord</u>" **Proverbs 18:22**

"Houses and riches are the inheritance of fathers: and <u>a **prudent wife** is from the Lord</u>" **Proverbs 19:14**KJV

A prudent wife has understanding, and she is wise. She adds to her husband's life and is a compliment to him. Not a troublemaker.

BE GENTLE.

CHAPTER 5

Wrong Man

Are you married to a man like Nabal? There was a man in the bible whose wife's name was Abigail.

1Samuel 25: 3KJV "Now the name of the man was Nabal; and the name of his wife was Abigail: and she was a woman of good understanding, and of a beautiful countenance: but the man was churlish and evil in his doings and he was of the house of Caleb."

Churlish: - means to be rude, impolite, ill-mannered or uncivil.

This man was evil, how on earth Abigail ended up marrying this man? **HOW DID YOU** end up marrying the man you married? What was done that you don't know about? What exchange was made?

David showed kindness to this man's shepherds and in a time of need David sent his servants to Nabal to ask of him food and water, and he refused. David was angry at this and intended to kill Nabal and that pertained to him, but Abigail intercepted him, after hearing how good David treated Nabal's shepherds.

Read the whole chapter of 1 Samuel 25.

This woman married a man that was the opposite of who she was.

Most likely it was an arranged marriage, I assume.

Abigail had respect for David, and she was God fearing, sacrificial and willing to give her life for the sake of saving others. God smote Nabal and he died, God returned his own wickedness upon his own head and delivered Abigail from this man forever. I can only imagine the cruelty she and the servants must have endured by Nabal's hand.

Being married to the wrong man can result in the cancelation of one's destiny.

This kind of man holding the position of being "the head" according to the scriptures or leader in your life can result in you, living a dying life.

I know of a few marriages that were entered into for the wrong reasons, some were for money, security, pregnancy, arranged by parents, jealousy, impatience, etc.

Jealousy and being impatient are what I'll speak on briefly.

I have heard of people getting married because their friends got married.

Why would anyone do this? It's like getting married was an epidemic back then, if you weren't married, you were look down on as an outcast. So, you hurry to find someone to marry and end up lonely and depressed instead.

True Short Stories

1. I know a woman that got married, the couple tried to have children for years and to no avail, the wife went through series of abandonment because her husband worked far away from home, not long after, she found out he was having an affair and had a child by another woman. That distant job and long hours were lies.

Why do these things happen? Did love fade? Was there even love to begin with?

2. I knew a woman that suffered at the hand of her abusive common-law husband and father of her children. I was told that he stuck a needle in her leg at one point in an attempt to paralyze her. She would seek help many times to leave him and he would do the same to have her stay with him and not leave. She finally left and married a better man.

3. I was at a friend's house one afternoon and we heard a big scream, when we all ran out the house my friend's drunken uncle stabbed his girlfriend in her eye with a machete.

4. A common law husband sexually molested his stepdaughter for years, as we heard the story unfold as the mother cried out in shock, she cried for days, but stayed with him and officially married him a few years later. (I'm just has lost as you are) but it happened.

5. There's this lady that has been engaged for years wearing a ring expecting to get married at some point but there's no wedding plans being made, she already had two children for her fiancé but on three different occasions, he would show up at the house, bringing home a child he fathered five of eight years ago for her to raise.

6. A man left his wife and kids for over ten years and returned with this statement.

"This house belongs to me I can return anytime."

How did these women end up with these men? Did they settle for Mr. Right now? Too impatient to wait on Mr. Right that God was preparing in His timing.

I remember being asked "are you dating, who is the lucky guy?" my reply would be "still waiting" and that person looked at me and said, "He will be worth the wait trust me". That is the most encouraging thing I've heard regarding this, because all I've heard is "you need to find somebody, you need to go to this or that conference or sign up on a dating website and you need to do this and that, you're getting old fast, and you should freeze your eggs".

Isn't God more than capable of bringing me in the presence of the man of His choice. I don't need to help God and I am not making the same mistake twice by looking on the outside. God knows the heart of man, He will send me the man with the good heart, a man that will put God first in all things." And so, ladies, I wait.

My testimony

In the year 2007, as I went to work each day, indecisive about the future of my past marriage I would often take off my wedding ring, on this week, off next week.

At this time, I was separated but wondering if this was the last separation before filing for divorce.

Each day it was a struggle, I didn't know if I was going or coming; I was at a crossroads. I kept a diary, a matter of fact I had (3) three, one I kept in my work bag, one that's always home and one that had no more pages left.

One day at work around noon, I wrote a letter to God, in the letter I told him all that I had gone through, the hurt, the abuse, the regret, confessing that I had made a mistake and how scared I was.

I told him I was tired of moving out and moving back in. I said God, please deliver me and send me a sign, I need to know what to do, I can't keep living like this and I want to be in your divine will. I don't want to make any decision that would make things worse for me, just tell me what to do, give me an answer today in Jesus name, I signed my name and closed the book.

I looked all day for a sign, there was no sign. I got myself together and closed up the store I worked at and was heading towards the main gate, someone called out to me, it was the security guard, he asked to speak to me for a minute I said "about what? I need to go" It was already dark, almost 7pm and I needed to catch the bus.

I thought he was going to waste my time. These were his exact words

"I've been watching you playing with your finger, are you married or not?"

I said " yes" **He said "you don't know what to do, your married to the wrong man. Right woman, wrong man! You are true to him, but he is not true to you, you do everything you're supposed to do but he still does wrong by you, right woman, wrong man!".** While he was saying these words, he started jumping and pointing at me saying **"<u>Your marriage was not ordained by God!</u> God did not choose this man for you; <u>you did not wait on God!</u> You chose this man and this marriage will never work! <u>Right woman, wrong man!</u> He cheats on you; he hurt and abuse you.... and mark my words <u>this marriage will never work</u> and if it does, I am a dead man!".** As he finished saying the last words, he used his index finger like a knife across his neck and still jumping back and forth. It's as if he couldn't stay still with this message any longer.

I was so frightened. I said, "who are you? and how do you know these things? why are you watching me?" he said " I am a man of God, I'm an Evangelist and God shows me things in dreams when I sleep and I see visions and I was supposed to come to you from last week but was not sure how to approach you but felt like I had to do it now". I began to cry, and I just walked away in shock. I didn't even remember the letter I wrote to God until the next day.

I personally was hesitant to put so much of my private past life out in the open but what if this can save someone's life, destiny, purpose? What if this book can save someone's MIND from tipping over the deep end? I felt like mine, went close to the edge before. **God answered me!! And it was clear and from that point on, my mind was made up to start moving on and never looking back.**

**SIGNS ARE ALWAYS CLEAR.
REMOVE THE CLUTTER.**

CHAPTER 6

Right Man

Every girl dream of marrying her prince charming, Mr. Right, the One. She knows exactly the kind of man she wants. But only God knows the kind of man she needs, that will be suitable for her talents, skill, intellect, passion and calling. Compatibility! my friends, is key. Being able to walk in agreement, be two people of one mind.

First of all, have God at the center of the relationship. When you don't understand your spouse, you go to God not your friend or your mother, go to the one that gave him to you, He understands him more than you do, He created him. The right man will see you; God will place you in his path. You are not to go looking for a man, you will come home with Mr. Wrong. Go about your business and God will make you and the man, he chose for you, cross paths.

Look at Ruth, she was minding her own business taking care of her Mother-in-law, she was genuinely trying to find food, humbly hoping to find grace in the site of Naomi's husband Elimelech's, kinsman Boaz, her intention was **not** for him to see her as a suitable wife.

Ruth found grace in the heart of Boaz because **she trusted the God of Israel**.

Ruth 2 :10 – 12KJV "She fell on her face, and bowed herself to the ground and said unto him, Why have I found grace in thine eyes, that thou shouldest take knowledge of me, seeing I am a stranger?....And Boaz answered and said unto her, It hath fully been showed me, all that thou hast done unto thy mother in law since the death of thine husband: and how thou hast left thy father and mother, and the land of thy nativity, and art come unto a people which thou knowest not heretofore…..The Lord recompence thy work, and a full reward be given thee of the Lord God of Israel, under whose wings thou art come to trust."

Ruth loved her Mother-in-law; she had a pure heart. Naomi told Ruth to go back to her people and unto her gods and she refused and chose to make Naomi's God her God. <u>God looks at the decisions we make</u>, not all the time will God tell you what to do because you won't do it from your heart but out of instruction, just to say you were obedient, but you really don't want to, that's why the Lord test us, to see what you will do, when you don't hear from him. That's when His written word is your guide and your conscience.

Does God have to tell you not to cheat on an exam? Or on your taxes? Or withhold your tithe and offering? Or pay back a loan? God is watching the independent decisions we make, and that is why we wait on him for clear confirmations of his perfect and good will for our lives.

We know the story how Ruth ended up marrying Boaz. There is Blessing in obedience from the heart, "……all that thou sayest unto me I will do" Ruth 3:5

The right man will do right by you. He will protect you, care about your whole person, provide for you, pray for you and one of his main priority is to make you happy and have a happy home.

Boaz "bought all that was Elimelech's and all that was to Chilion and Mahlon, of the hand of Naomi. Moreover, Ruth the Moabitess, the wife of Mahlon, have I purchased to be my wife………"**Ruth 4:9-11KJV**

When the right man comes, he will do all that is in his power to ensure that you are taken care of.

I wondered why God allowed all three of those husbands to die. When I read the scripture, it states that Elimelech took his wife Naomi and their two sons Mahlon and Chilion from Bethlehem-Judah and brought them into Moab, a country of idol worshippers of the god of Chemosh, these worshippers did human sacrifices of children and babies. After reading I concluded that this could possibly be the reason, his two sons disobeyed God's word in marrying women from Moab. But why was Naomi spared? Maybe she didn't want to go in the first place, but she had no choice. And her desire was not to find a man there but to return to Bethlehem-Judah.

When you marry the wrong man, sometimes you have no choice but to go along with what he is doing but praying secretly and keeping the faith that someday your deliverance will come because God knows your heart. But God will still acknowledge him as the head.

God did not give Naomi another husband but through the seed of a right man and a loyal daughter in law, God gave her a child to raise as her own.

When the right man shows up, he will love only you.

*In Genesis 29:18KJV "And **Jacob loved** Rachel; and said, I will serve thee seven years for Rachel thy younger daughter.'* In verse 20 it states that *"And he served seven years for Rachel; and they seemed unto him but a few days, for **the love** he had to her"*.

When you read this story how Jacob was beguiled into marrying Leah, he was so hurt and disappointed because he wanted who he loved and served for, no other could substitute. He served another seven years for Rachel, and when he had fulfilled, he was given Rachel to be his wife.

"And he went in also unto Rachel, and he loved Rachel more than Leah, and served with him seven other years" **Genesis 29 :30**

Rachel had to wait (14) fourteen years for a man she knew was her future husband, he had to work for her. The right man will put the work in to have you by his side.

It wasn't fair to Leah to be given to a man that didn't desire her but according to custom in that country and time, the first born is married first then the youngest. And God was merciful towards her when he saw she was hated and opened her womb.

God looks at the heart.

BE YOU, AND THE ONE FOR YOU, WILL LOVE ALL OF WHO YOU REALLY ARE.

CHAPTER 7

Wrong Woman

"And the Lord God said, it is not good that the man should be alone; I will make him a helpmeet for him." **Genesis 2:18 KJV**

"And the Lord caused a deep sleep to fall upon Adam, and he slept: and he took one of his ribs, and closed up the flesh instead thereof.

"And the rib which the Lord God had taken from the man, made he a woman, and brought her unto the man"

And Adam said, this is now bone of my bones, and flesh of my flesh: she shall be called Woman, because she was taken out of man" **Genesis 2:21-23KJV**

"For the man is not of the woman, but the woman of the man"

"Neither was the man created for the woman but the woman for the man".

1Corinthians 11:8 – 9KJV

Now with that understood, I can clearly state that women that wants to rule their husbands, have the last say all the time and manipulate their husbands into doing what they want to do, you are not in right standing with God.

Some women, if they don't get their way, as punishment they would withhold themselves from their husbands. You are operating outside of the will of God and operating in the spirit of rebellion and error.

If you've married the wrong man who is to be blamed?

By observation most woman are extremely curious, most of us like to know what's going on, even things that does not concern us and most women like to talk.

We want to be heard even if it's not that serious.

Many times, we blame the man we chose. It was not God that gave us the person we are with, we chose to be with that person and when we realize they're not what we thought they would be, we try to change them.

We start telling our spouse what to do and how to do it and why. Some women use their bodies and beauty or their children as leverage, in an effort to change their husband to become what he is not and will never be, because he is just not that kind of man.

The whole idea of thinking you can change a man is a BIG LIE from satan.

The man has to desire a change in the first place and make the decision to change without you having to do anything, most women are guilty of this. Men are just as guilty, but they do it in a different way.

Sometimes for peace sake and to stop you from nagging, men will fall into a trap and give into a woman's nag and end up destroying his whole life.

Let's look at Adam and Eve

"And the man said, the woman whom thou gavest to be with me, she gave me of the tree, and I did eat……And the LORD God said unto the woman,

what is this that thou hast done? And the woman said. The <u>serpent beguiled me</u>, and I did eat." **Genesis 3:12 -13. KJV**

"Unto the woman he said, I will greatly multiply thy sorrow and thy conception; in sorrow thou shalt bring forth children; and thy desire shall be to thy husband, and he shall have **RULE** over thee." Genesis 3:16 KJV

The word <u>beguiled</u> according to Merriam Webster.com means; to lead by deception

Are women still being beguiled by this serpent? To desire rule over their husbands, and constantly criticizing the man. Are you under the influence of the same serpent that beguiled Eve?

Eve knew they were not supposed to eat it. Did she tell Adam what fruit it was, or could it be, that she just gave it to him and said, "Here honey have a piece of fruit" and without hearing the dialogue between her and the serpent or even thinking twice about it, because he trusted her, Adam took a bite and ate without knowledge of the tree it came from and to his surprise it was the fruit from the tree of life, because now, we are naked. Could this be how it played out?

*"And unto Adam he said, because thou hast hearken to the **VOICE** of thy **wife**, and hast eaten of the tree, of which I commanded thee saying, thou shalt not eat it: cursed is the ground for thy sake; in sorrow shalt thou eat of it all the days of thy life".* **Genesis 3:17 KJV**

Did Adam really know that the fruit he was being offered to eat was the tree of life? It was Eve's voice telling him to have some, and he listened to her. She is the one that listened to the serpent Satan, she chose to believe the lie and desired to be wise. Desiring to be wise is a good thing but wisdom is not gained by being disobedient to God. You can't out smart God. Does that mean she thought she wasn't wise? Eve looked at the tree, saw that it was pleasant to the eyes and desired it and deliberately disobeyed God's commandment.

I'm not writing this book to bash anyone, man or woman. This book is being written by the grace of God to hopefully stop someone from making one of the worst mistakes of their lives or to help deliver a person that is presently going through a denial or manipulation.

A woman was created with her own purpose, preferences, identity, role, destiny and function that God has given her.

She has specific skills to effectively help the man she was destined to be with and carry his seed into the world, with careful nurturing and support, teaching them alongside her husband the way of the Lord. A married woman is supposed to help her husband build, she is to support him, respect him and encourage him, be his confidant. She is not a sex slave, a breeder, just a seed carrier or a yes woman. Women are comforters, gentle encouragers, teachers, counselors and bold warriors that will defend their home. They protect as well as they desire to be protected. Their desire is to have a happy marriage and family but most importantly to please God by fulfilling her God given purpose as an individual, married or not.

1Corinthians 7- 34KJV

"....... but she that is married careth for the things of the world, how she may please her husband".

A woman that seeks only to please herself is not suitable for marriage, the marriage foundation is first, God, love and commitment and without love you cannot commit. A woman that is self-centered can ruin a man's life.

Let's look at Jezebel and Ahab.

Ahab was the king of Israel, and he went and marry Jezebel a Zidonian, the daughter of Ethbaal, they were idol worshippers of Baal. This wife was not right for Ahab because she led him further away from God and deeper into sin, she took matters in her own hands by killing God's prophets and installing her false prophets of Baal, Ahab does nothing to stop her because he has already been seduced by her enchantments. Yes, she was a witch.

"And it came to pass, when Joram saw Jehu, that he said, Is it peace, Jehu?" And he answered and said, "What peace, so long as the whoredoms of <u>thy mother Jezebel</u> and <u>her witchcrafts</u> are so many". **2 Kings 9 -22.KJV**

When a man marries a woman that serves satan, she will rule over him, everything that is supposed to honor God in marriage is done the opposite way. The man plays the wife role, and the woman plays the man role. She makes all the decisions and has the final say and the man is just silently doing what he is told, he becomes a robot. He is ordered around and treated with no respect. If he tries to have any say, he is shut down with threats and even physically attacked.

Some women manipulate men into marrying them, placing substance in their food or drink or using pregnancy.

Jezebel, Ahab's wife took matters in her own hands when Ahab told her that Naboth refused to give him the inheritance of his father. She organized to have Naboth killed, she was a cold-blooded premeditated murderer. She planned it so well, using her husband's authority <u>unknown</u> to him.

Again, here you see a woman that thinks she should be in charge, doing things without her husband's knowledge, thinking that she is helping him, trying to prove that she can play his role by using his authority to carry out her evil plot, all in the name of helping him out. In other words, what you don't have the guts to do, I'll do, I just need your stamp on it, but you don't have to know that.

That's Manipulation at its best.

1Kings 21 8 – 10 KJV

"<u>So, she wrote letters in Ahab's name</u> and <u>sealed them with his seal</u> and sent them to the elders and nobles that were in his city, dwelling with Naboth."

And she wrote in the letters saying, Proclaim a fast and <u>set Naboth on</u> high among the people.

And set two men, sons of Belial, before him to bear witness against him, saying Thou didst blaspheme God and the king. And Then carry him out and stone him that he may die".

Jezebel was a liar, and she did it well. Her effort of helping her husband always ends up hurting him even worse, she ruined his reputation and brought judgment upon her whole house.

Ahab is completely under her spell….

1Kings21:15- 16 KJV

"And it came to pass, when Jezebel heard that Naboth was stoned, and was dead that Jezebel said to Ahab, Arise, take possession of the vineyard of Naboth the Jezreelite, which he refused to give thee for money: for Naboth is not alive, but dead.

And it came to pass, when Ahab heard that Naboth was dead, that Ahab rose up to go down to the vineyard of Naboth the Jezreelite, to take possession of it."

Right away the word of God came to the Prophet Elijah the Tishbite telling him to go down to meet Ahab and to give him a message. God addressed **the man first**, that should tell us something. Ahab was not the one that conspired and killed Naboth, but God gave the prophet Elijah a direct message of rebuke and judgement for Ahab.

1Kings 21:19-20 KJV

"And thou shalt speak unto him, saying, Thus saith the Lord, Hast thou killed and also taken possession?………in the place where dogs licked the blood of Naboth shall dogs lick thy blood, even thine…. because thou hast **sold thyself** to work evil in the sight of the Lord."

Again, a man faced severe consequences because of his wife's actions. Ahab didn't refuse what his wife brought to him, he didn't disapprove of her dealings, and he didn't inquire. It was the <u>decision</u> Ahab made to go take Naboth's Vineyard that brought the judgment on his house. <u>Our decisions are life and death.</u>

"But there was none like unto Ahab, which did sell himself to work wickedness in the sight of the Lord, <u>whom Jezebel his wife stirred up</u>" **1Kings 21:25KJV**

Ahab's wife persuaded him to worship idols and do wickedness, he turned his back on God because of a woman.

So did Solomon in **1Kings 11:1 – 3KJV**

"But king Solomon loved many <u>strange women</u>, together with the daughter of Pharaoh, women of the Moabites, Ammonites, Edomites, Zidonians and Hittites ….2 Of the nations concerning which the Lord said unto to the children of Israel, Ye shall not go in to them neither shall they come in unto you for <u>surety they will turn away your heart after their gods</u>: Solomon clave unto these in love.…..3 And he had seven hundred wives, princesses and three hundred concubines: <u>and his wives turned away his heart.</u>"

Men, marry a woman that draws you closer to God, a woman that is just as passionate about the things of God as you are. You cannot do anything together unless you agree, one will pull the other in the direction they are going or there will be a separation.

Solomon lost his kingdom. The wisest man that ever lived, was seduced and manipulated by his idol worshipping wives.

Samson lost his superhuman strength because he loved and went in unto the wrong women, they enticed him and lied.

<u>The plan of the enemy is to steal and kill your destiny and this is a sure way to do it.</u>

The devil will partner you up with a child of the devil, set you up to marry a man or a woman that wants YOU but NOT your God. They will take such good care of you dutifully, take you to church even encourage you to go, why? Because you are safe to be with, there's no worry about you being unfaithful.

Satan will trick you into marrying someone that has a form of Godliness, a believer in the Gospel but never truly commits, a church attendee but not a true born-again Christian.

Many that are married today will not remain married because the motive was wrong. I knew someone that told me she only got married so she could travel out of the country, even though she was in the relationship for more than five years before, but that was her reason to get married, so she could show ties to the country that she had reason to return.

In Esther 1:12 KJV

Queen Vashti disobeyed the king's command, disrespected her husband, by rejecting his request in front of an entire kingdom. This was an open display of rebelliousness, stubbornness and a show to prove power and defiance.

Maybe she thought to herself, I'm queen Vashti, how dare you request me while I'm putting on a feast and entertaining my guest. **Little did she know her actions offended the entire kingdom.**

Esther 1:16 KJV "And Memucan answered before the king and the princes, Vashti the queen hath **not** done wrong to the King **only**, but also to all the princes, and to all the people that are in all the provinces of the king Ahasuerus".

Wives when you dishonor your husband, you dishonor his God given leadership to govern the family and all that he is responsible for, by God's direction, you dishonor God's order. Queen Vashti was removed from her royal estate, and another better that her was made Queen instead. According to **Esther 1:19 KJV**

What the Lord did **<u>not</u>** join together, He can surely pull apart, for surely the Lord chose Esther to take Vashti's place. But who knows, if Queen Vashti was a humble and wise wife and queen to her husband and King, maybe God could have granted deliverance to the Jews another way. God exalts the humble and rejects the proud.

Being off balance is a strain.

A LIFE OF BURDEN IS NOT THE WILL OF GOD.

CHAPTER 8

Marriage Hoax

Many persons like the idea of being married, but do not want the commitment. Some are completely clueless to the responsibility of the role they will play within the marriage institution.

They get married for the wrong reason. Some marry to be accepted, some for procreation, some to please parents, for truce, for financial security, to keep tradition, to hide a secret life, you name it.

Then you have the marriages that are literal traps. I was hesitant to write about this, but the Holy Spirit just kept reminding me how important this would be to someone. Both men and women use witchcraft to manipulate a desired person to agree to marry them. This REAL!

Are you married to someone you have **no interest** in and is still wondering, how did I marry this person?

You were not even friends to begin with, it's as if, it just happened, or your ex-boyfriend popped up out the blue, telling you he wants to get married, but for years he's been telling you, he has no interest in marriage. You might have seen a person occasionally, met once or twice, had dinner once and the next thing is, you're planning a wedding but deep down inside you are still not interested, hoping that will change.

The red flags were there but it's as if they were invisible at the time but now, you're seeing them bright and clear, when it's too late. You've already said "I do" to a stranger or to someone you have no interest in and at the end of the wedding you begin to wonder how I got here? and why am I not resisting?

True short story

A Lady I would call by the name of Sharyn (not her real name) She was seeing this guy and for a while they were intimate and established a relationship for some years. However, Sharyn accepted Christ as her personal savior and became a born-again Christian, she wrote her boyfriend a letter informing him of her life changes and commitment to Christ and to let him know, she has to end this relationship and that he should move on. After not hearing from him for a while, she got a reply that he had gotten baptized and that he wanted to marry her.

Now Sharyn not being matured enough, believed this was enough to make such a long-term life decision by agreeing to get married to him. This guy never spoke about serving God or anything Christ like, there was no interest. They got married and Sharyn lived an unhappy life of 20 +years enduring many episodes of domestic violence. This man was never committed to God, he stopped going to church, he refused for years to have a child with Sharyn (his wife) that desperately wanted to have children.

Sharyn filed for divorce after she had gotten over the fear of what people were going to say about her.

There comes a time in our lives when you must have a "I don't care anymore" attitude about what people will say, but rather do what is right for you. Before we can love anyone, we must first love ourselves.

That is why Jesus said, *"love your neighbor **as yourself**"* Mark 12:31.

1. Love God 2. Love Yourself 3. Love others

Wisdom must have its place; we are made in his image and God is wise. Therefore, He expects us to use the wisdom He has given us. Wisdom is knowing what to **do.**

"Prudent man forseeth the evil, and hideth himself; but the simple pass on, and are punished". **Proverbs 27:12 KJV**

Jesus Christ is the perfect example of using wisdom. *"Jesus said unto them, verily, verily, I say unto you, Before Abraham was, I Am……Then took they up stones to cast at him: but Jesus hid himself, and went out of the Temple, going through the midst of them and so passed by"* **John 8:58KJV**

Mother- in- Laws

Some of us are blessed with wonderful in-laws. You meet officially at a family outing or dinner, and you are genuinely welcomed into the family, with a toast to new beginnings. Not so with some of us.

Mother in laws are very protective of their sons, from my observation and experience, unless they were never close. Some will go to great lengths to ensure he is treated right in their opinion and your best will never be enough in their mind.

Make sure to do your background check on his or her family. Observe your future partner's behavior around them especially their mother. Is he respectful to his mother? Is she and her Mom loud? Are they impatient with their parents? Is he/she helpful, because they could be the complete opposite around you, just to keep you, but one day they will get tired of the pretense and begin to show their true self and guess what! Their mother and the rest of their family will support him or her and your left alone.

Your fiancé could be a committed Christian, but their mother and the rest of the family are unsaved, or they could be of a different religion or worst, they possibly could be flat out Anti-Christ or involved in witchcraft.

Your priority is to find out what you're getting yourself into and to make sure you're in the divine will of God. Because in some culture and religion, arranged marriages for their sons and daughters are set before they even reach puberty. Marrying outside of their race and religion is forbidden and detested. But here you go trying to marry her son or have married him without her blessing, Honey, you're in for the fight of your life, like you've never seen, both naturally and spiritually. They will come for you in your dreams, they'll cause all types of misunderstanding and strife to break up your marriage. Don't go tying the knot before meeting the parents or having full knowledge of who they are.

<u>Beware of the unsaved, ungodly mother- in- law, the wolf in sheep's clothing.</u>

An unsaved mother in-law will do wickedness with good intentions out of ignorance to ensure her son's or daughter's marriage is secure. But instead of peace, love, harmony and understanding your life is full of misery, war, hate and regret. All because of someone who may be meddling in your marriage. Her meddling could be her words of dislike towards you as a person, disapproval of the marriage in general or her secret sorceries in the night to destroy your marriage in the day.

<u>Beware of the controlling Mother-in-law</u>

This mother-in-law is selfish, she manipulates her son, her son is her handy man, business partner, plumber, caregiver and friend. He hardly has time for his own family, and he cannot seem to respectfully say "no" to Mom. Her real husband (the father) just works, bring his paycheck to her, he eats, sleeps and watch TV. She does everything else. She is the leader of the house, and her husband follows her.

Beware of the hunting Mother-in-law.

She is looking for a husband or a wife for her daughter or son and she wants the best, but is her daughter or son the best for you? Make sure not to be pressured into marrying anyone that seems to be so available by their parents, they might be looking to get someone to take them off their hands. He or she could be mentally ill, terminally ill or financially irresponsible and they can't bear the burden anymore.

CHAPTER 9

Your Children

Sometimes children from a union <u>not</u> ordained by God tends to be troublesome, rebellious, sick or simply living a life as a result of their parents' bad choices. In order for that child to have a life he or she has to accept Jesus Christ as his personal savior and seek deliverance from generational curses and live a committed Christian life. Reprogramming thoughts, patterns and unhealthy habits that would result in making the same bad choices his/her parents made.

For example, Doctors have advised partners that has full blown sickle cell not to have children, they will not produce healthy children, or the child might die, and the mother might die in child's birth, it's severely high risk. It's the same risk we take joining ourselves with individuals that God has not given to us. We take the risk that might kill our dreams, or might cancel our destinies, minimize our potentials, our gifts suffer, and so does the children produced from such relationships and marriages God did not ordained to be, but allowed in His permissive will because he gave us a **free will, the freedom of choice.**

Let's look at Abraham. Why didn't God stop Abraham from going in unto Hagar?

Sara gave her husband her handmaid to be his wife *"And Sarai Abram's wife took Hagar her maid the Egyptian, after Abram had dwelt ten years in the land of Canaan and gave to her husband Abram to be wife....... And he went in unto Hagar, and she conceived............"* **Genesis 16:3-4. KJV**

God did not stop Abram. He allowed it, but was that God's perfect and divine will? **No.**

God already told Abram and Sarah what his divine will was but because of <u>impatience</u> they thought they could help God along, by giving Him a more realistic way of bringing His word to pass, because they couldn't understand how this conception was possible given the circumstance.

Hagar had Ishmael, he is Abram's first son, but God did not establish his covenant with Ishmael, that came from his permissive will. It was with the **son of promise** that came from Sarah's womb, Isaac. You <u>cannot</u> force God to bless what He did not ordain or approve of. Ishmael's prophesy was completely different from Isaac's.

When the Lord promises you something or gives you a command it will always appear impossible, unattainable and sometimes ridiculous. Sarah laughed, didn't she? God told Moses to <u>*speak*</u> to the rock, correct? Anything God tells you to do will require faith in God and patience.

Through the prophet Elisha God instructed Naaman to dip in the river Jordan seven times. At first Naaman was confused and upset with this approach, but he was counseled to yield, and he did in 2Kings 5:14.

The third time he dipped, he probably thought that this is nonsense. But he continued to dip by faith, patiently, and as ridiculous as it may seem, he received his miraculous healing.

Faith in God brings the supernatural to the natural realm called miracles. We don't know what was going on during those seven dips, but we sure can tell what happen when he came up out the water the seventh time. The word of God shall accomplish that which it was sent. It shall come to pass.

The children that pay for the sins of their fathers

All seventy sons of Ahab were killed, all in the one day. There was none that remained of the house of Ahab, because of his wickedness with his wife Jezebel.

Rehoboam son of King Solomon became king after his father. Remember earlier I showed you where Solomon turned from God when he began to marry those strange women that worshipped idols. This was a result of his actions. His son lost the respect of the children of Israel, and they rebelled against his rule because he made life harder for them. There was a split amongst the tribes that was prophesied by the prophet Ahijah, because of their idol worship and God divided the kingdom. Jeroboam son of Nabat, a servant of King Solomon became the first King of the divided northern Kingdom of Israel. He also made Israel sin.

Your children might suffer and bare your consequence too. If they don't stop and make a right turn towards God and seek him diligently. The wrong path will lead them deeper towards self-destruction. When you are choosing a partner don't think only about you but consider if this person is suitable to help you raise your children in the right way, that is pleasing unto God.

CHAPTER 10

Wicked Affections

"Woe to them that devise iniquity and work evil upon their beds! when the morning is light, they practice it, because it is in the power of their hand."

Micah 2:1KJV

A lot of persons are in relationships/marriages against their will, but they are not aware of it, because spiritually they are in a cage in their minds, being manipulated by the use of witchcraft and sorcery.

Acts 8:9-11KJV *"But there was a certain man, called Simon which before time in the same city <u>used sorcery and bewitched the people</u> of Samaria, giving out that himself was some great one: …. **To whom they all gave heed, from the least to the greatest, saying, this man is the great power** of God…. And to him they had regard, because that of <u>**longtime he had bewitched them with sorceries**</u>".*

Do you see this here? *"Of a long time"* many of us have been under a spell for <u>decades.</u> **It's time to wake up, snap out of it** and RUN!! IN THE NAME OF JESUS CHRIST!

Many people are looking for love in the wrong places. They visit mediums and palm readers, psychics, spiritual readers to name the least. They seek to find love, to rekindle the flame of a relationship, summon a past lover or ex-husband or ex-wife back in their lives. This is wrong, this is wickedness, this is sinful, this is evil.

Witchcraft is controlling a person or a situation using manipulations and intimidations, both of which can be empowered by the use of the dark arts.

Act 13:8-10KJV *"But Elymas the sorcerer (for so is his name by interpretation) withstood them, seeking to turn away the deputy from the faith. 9 Then Saul (who also is called Paul), filled with the Holy Ghost, set his eyes on him. And said, O full of all subtility and all mischief, thou child of the devil, thou enemy of all righteousness, wilt thou not cease to pervert the right ways of the lord."*

This has now become a common place practice. It's advertised on TV. There are flyers on public transportation. It's easily accessed, gone are the days when you had to know a person that, knows somebody that secretly practiced casting spells. How to cast a spell and put a curse on someone is on the internet and the secret society is no longer a secret. What is right is seen as wrong and what is wrong is accepted as right.

Today Marriages are being redefined by lawmakers of this world. I chose to keep Marriage sacred unto God, the creator of the marriage institution between one man and one woman divinely joined together by Him. This book is to warn you or prepare you.

The one for you is out there, but there is only one, and he or she is the only **<u>right</u>** one. The one that is of **God's choice.** Not your parent's choice or close friends or even your choice. Don't be easily swept off your feet. Give it time. God requires you to **wait**. God's choice is the best. This person will not be all together perfect, but they will be the right person for you.

Friends be mindful that this person will have flaws but for the most part they will be perfect in God's eyes for you, and the love that God placed in them for you will be yours only and he or she will **<u>accept</u>** you for who God created you to be.

I believe the right one will fit in your life like a missing puzzle piece you've been looking for.

CHOOSE GOD'S CHOICE

CHAPTER 11

Domestic Violence

This is a serious and sensitive problem. In this situation, everyone is a victim and believe it or not sometimes we create these issues ourselves. This is a horrible thing to experience, it's like living with a monster. It's not to be taken lightly or considered a common thing.

Our own poor decisions have cost us to pay a very high price. Sometimes we ignore the red flags, we make excuses, we blame ourselves and others.

But more often than none it takes us by surprise. It came out of nowhere and the battle begins, and you were not prepared. I was not prepared at all. This is a force of darkness that is assigned to kill you. If it cannot succeed physically after it's many attempts, then it will try in every other way possible. This is a destiny assassin. Its orders are to remove your mind from pursuing your God given purpose. So, with this trauma you're depressed, full of anxiety, fearful, suicidal, angry, bitter, ashamed, doubtful, hopeless and purposeless.

I want to encourage someone today; YOU HAVE A PURPOSE!

You are fearfully and wonderfully made by *God He took time to create you*. You were not created in a hurry or made in a mass production factory. You are one of a kind, cut to perfection, refined in completion, polished to a shine.

Jesus Christ loves you unconditionally and His arms are wide open to hug you and love you. If only you would just accept Him in your heart. Accept His love and embrace it. He paid a high price to redeem you. Accept God's love through Jesus Christ His Son and be free of all the fear and shame and begin your PURPOSE **FULL** LIFE!

It is not the will of God for you to live a life that is not pleasing to Him. Living in a home where you are repeatedly or occasionally experiencing domestic violence is not the will of God for your life. This goes for both men and women.

A relationship is to meet the need for companionship, friendship and commitment that hopefully will lead to marriage, which will continue in the marriage union.

When you see a man beats a woman to a pulp with little or no remorse what do you call that? or a woman that slaps her husband in the face for any reason? That is NOT of God. That's a demonic force operating in or through that person and the person doing harm needs deliverance. Nobody should live like that especially in a marriage where you are to be cared for more than anywhere else.

Some men can be very controlling and abusive. They think you can't live without them because they took you from your parent's house and you have nowhere else to go. He knows where you work, where the kids go to school, where you go to church, he knows where your friends live. You have no money; everything is in his name. He threatens you "If you try to leave me again, I will kill you". You can't blame everything on the devil, people have a free will, and they know what they are saying and doing while being <u>influenced by darkness</u>. They just give up their will to the dark side, that's what happens.

In movies we see women slapping men in the face and throwing their drink in the man's face at a dinner table, before leaving when he says something rude, wouldn't it be fair and appropriate to respond by saying something that will let the man know not to speak to you like that, rather than setting a bad example and sending a wrong message, that it's ok for women to hit men or publicly insult him and expect him not to react.

ALL human beings must control their emotions.

One of the worst things about this situation, is when your cry for help is ignored by neighbors, family members, and sometimes friends, it's as if it became their norm. After a while they look away and pretend, they don't see the bruises, thinking if you're staying in that, it must be what you want, but little do they know, how badly you want to leave but you feel trapped. The persons close to you sometimes are not the ones that normally help you. It's the people that you're not in close relations with, they're the ones that shows more genuine concern and offer to help.

I'm a survivor of this, so I must give God all THE GLORY which He deserves, He was my ROCK. He still is. Jesus Christ my friend that sticks closer than a brother. He was my strength in those days when I asked God to take me out of this world in my sleep, because I felt I had nothing to live for, I woke up surprise I was still alive.

When God placed purpose in you, nothing can take you out of this world before your time, as a child of God. God will bring to pass the word he spoke over your life before you were even born, and His word cannot return void.

"So shall my word be that goeth forth out of my mouth: it shall not return unto me void, but it shall accomplish that which I please, and it shall prosper in the thing whereto I sent it." Isaiah 55:11KJV

"Before I formed you in the womb, I knew you, before you were born, I set you apart; I appointed you as a prophet to the nations." Jeremiah 1:5KJV

CHAPTER 12

Submit to Love

The word submit according to Merriam Webster.com means: to yield to governance or authority.

God is the all wise God, and if He commands the wife to submit to her husband, there is a wise and divine principle intact that governs the wife's position as the helpmate. Wives you are submitting to God in your husband. It is God that is leading him.

Colossians 3:18-19 *"Wives, submit yourselves unto your own husbands, as it is fit in the Lord. 19.... **Husbands love your wives** and be not bitter against them".*

Let's look at what hinders submission.

An attitude of superiority, secret agenda, desire to rule and control, to manipulate for self-glorification to name a few. This will cause you to refuse instruction and wise counsel. A proud person cannot submit to any authority, not even God and that is why He rejects them, debase them and **exalts the humble**.

Submission starts with God.

A husband that is not submitted to God will be difficult to submit to, because he submits to no one but himself, in this case her submission is limited.

"….as it is fit in the lord" **Colossians 3:18-19.**

<u>God expects us to be wise.</u> Are you going to submit to a man that is telling you to go and prostitute yourself to help him with the bills? Or help him steal from the grocery store due to the fact that your role is to help? Is God saying stay in an abusive marriage and submit to your husband even when he beats you and humiliates you but only in private? NO! The word of God will not be used to promote disobedience and wickedness.

Husbands, if you are not submitted to God first and you are being led by your flesh and selfishness and not God and His word, you are not ready to lead a wife and a family.

Husbands if your wife is not submitted to God, she CANNOT submit to you. You are loving the wrong woman.

Proverbs 25: *"It is better to dwell in a corner of the house-top than with a brawling woman and in a wide house."*

Proverbs 21:19 *"It is better to dwell in the wilderness, than with a contentious and angry woman."* No one wants to be around continuous strife and quarrelling. <u>*It's not of God.*</u>

*"For where envying and strife is, there is confusion and **every evil work**."*

James 3:16

<u>Submission is a love language</u>. When you both are submitted to God, it's natural to love, and submission **responds to love**, it's readily given in entirety. Submission was not meant to be hard. As your husband lovingly asks you to do something, your response will be in loving submission to his request. As you both have faith and trust in God, together all will be well.

Wives you are not beneath your husbands, you are equal to him, functioning in a specific capacity that only you can fill. It's yours, own it.

A submissive wife has her husband's respect, it brings them closer. He can trust her to be his team player. He depends on her loyalty; her submission makes him feel secure.

Sarah submitted to her husband Abraham and honored him even in how she addressed him by calling him "lord", written with all lower caps. This is a **title of respect** in the Hebrew culture.

If you are married to an unsaved or disobedient man, the word of God advises that your attitude and your conversation is what may lead them to Christ.

"Likewise, ye wives, be in subjection to your own husbands; that if any obey not the word, they also may without the word be won by the conversation of the wives." ***1Peter 3:1***

Love her with the love of God

*"Whoso findeth a wife findeth **a good** thing,
and obtaineth favor of the Lord"*
Proverbs 18:22
*"House and riches are the inheritance of fathers:
and a **prudent** wife is from the Lord"*
Proverbs 19:14

"Who can find a virtuous woman? For her price is far above rubies. ***The heart of her husband doth safely trust in her****, so that he shall have no need of spoil. She will do him <u>good</u> and not evil all the days of her life..........."* 26 *"She openeth her mouth with <u>wisdom</u>; and in her tongue is the <u>law of kindness</u>. She looketh well to the ways of her household, and eateth not the bread of idleness." ......*30 *"Favor is deceitful, and beauty is vain: but a woman that feareth the Lord, she shall be praised."*
Proverbs 31: 10,26 and 30

*"Husbands, love your wives, even as Christ also
loved the church and gave himself for it"*
Ephesians 5:25KJV

A marriage is supposed to be where love and respect thrives. A life of continuous unity and strengthening each other in all facets of life. The role of the husband is to love, protect, provide and lead his wife, as head of her life (under Jesus Christ). It is his responsibility to contribute to her spiritual growth. "For the husband is the head of the wife" **Ephesians 5:23KJV**

"So, ought men to love their wives as their own bodies. He that loveth his wife loveth himself". Ephesians 5:28KJV

A husband that treats his God given wife badly, disregards her love and respect for him, and uses his authority against her, is in violation of God's holy word. When God placed her in your care it was **not** for her to replace your mother or become your maid.

She was carefully crafted to suite your need, your customized help mate.

God has entrusted you with the task of building her up and establishing her purpose on the earth as she helps you to establish yours. She needs love, and you are the one God has chosen to give her that love; you are the instrument through which God uses to provide that kind of physical expression of love through.

When you have found your wife ***that God has chosen***, instantly you will desire to love her. Love her with the imperfections even more unconditionally, as you love her with His love.

CHAPTER 13

Are you in Agreement?

"Can two walk together except they be agreed?" **Amos 3:3KJV**

In order for a husband and wife to live in harmony they must be in agreement. Disagreements will arise, but at the end, there must me an agreement. Because God has called us to peace.

If your unbelieving spouse leaves, then let them leave, in such cases you are not in bondage.

God is love and He is of peace. His word says *"…. seek peace and pursue it".*

Psalm 34:14KJV

We know how God feels about divorce and his desire for reconciliation, but there are rare exceptions.

In Malachi 2:16

"God hates putting away" but this has its place. Let's look at the book of Ezra, chapters 9 and10.

The children of Israel trespassed against God, by marrying strange wives of the land. Ezra prayed and confessed their sins to God seeking how they could make amends.

*"And now, O our God, what shall we say after this? for we have forsaken thy commandments, …Which thou hast commanded by thy servants the prophets, saying the land unto which ye go to possess it, is an unclean land with the filthiness of the people of the lands, with their abominations, which have filled it from one end to another with their uncleanness. 12. Now therefore **give not** your daughters unto their sons, **neither take their daughters** unto your sons, nor seek their peace or their wealth forever: <u>**that ye may be strong**</u>................" Ezra 9:10-12KJV*

Ezra 10 :2 -5 KJV *"And Shechaniah the son of Jehiel, one of the sons of Elam, answered and said unto Ezra, We have trespassed against our God, and have taken strange wives of the people of the land: yet now there is hope in Israel concerning this thing…. Now therefore let us make a **covenant with our God to put away all the wives**, and such as are born of them, according to the counsel of my lord, and of those that tremble at the commandment of our God; and let it be done according to the law. …. Arise; for this matter belongeth unto thee: we also will be with thee: be of good courage and do it…. Then arose Ezra, and made the chief priests, the Levites, and all **Israel, to swear that they should do according to this word**. And they sware".*

God knows why he gives us commandments, it's really for our good, our advantage, our safety and purity. There is no unity with conflict, no togetherness with division.

Influence is paramount. The company you keep has an effect on you, whether you know it or not. The persons you are in constant contact with contributes to your decision-making process. Unless you have completely separated yourself mentally from them, their influence has some degree of effect on your life. It will either make you or break you.

True short story

I heard of a woman trying to make a run for it, she had taken a cab over to her friend's house fleeing from her drunken abusive husband, and as she was re-telling her prior events to her friend, here comes her husband outside the house, yelling her name out in the late hours of the night, demanding the friend to release his wife to him. It was embarrassing and frightening.

She was afraid but to calm him down, she had to go with him. That's not the kind of person you want to be around, <u>such an influence can break you down to nothing</u>. In the following months she was pregnant, she had another child for him and when the friend would visit, she was always sad, poorly dressed and complained about the constant fights. Years later she ran away from him again, leaving the children behind to where he didn't have any contact with her and filed for divorce.

<u>Wrong relationships</u>

They weaken your potential, places a strain on you, it's like carrying a heavy load all the days of your life. It will hinder you from completely fulfilling your God's given destiny.

Ezra 10: 3,10,11 and 12.KJV

*"3 Now therefore let us make a covenant with our God to put away all the wives, and such as are born of them, according to the counsel of my lord and of those that tremble at the commandment of our God; <u>and let it be done according to the law</u>............................ 10 And Ezra the priest stood up and said unto them, Ye have transgressed, and have taken strange wives, to increase the trespass of Israel. 11 Now therefore make confession unto the Lord God of your fathers and<u> do his pleasure</u>: and **separate yourselves from the people of the land**, and from **the strange wives.12** Then all the congregation answered and said with a loud voice, as thou hast said, so must we do".*

The Israelites were not in agreement with their spouses or God. Ezra interceded for them or else God in his fury would have eventually punished them for their Idolatry severely.

So, they agreed to be separated from their heathen wives. <u>In this case it was the right thing to do</u>.

You see the presence of God will not continue to dwell among you, while you live in deliberate disobedience to His commandments and worst, blending holy with the abominable. The evil spirits of the heathen wives were cohabiting with God's people and influencing them to sin more and more.

"Be ye not unequally yoked together with unbelievers: for what fellowship hath righteousness with unrighteousness? <u>And what communion hath light with darkness?</u>". ***2 Corinthians 6:14 – 17KJV***

There are so many cases of exception this one I know personally.

Names of characters changed to protect privacy.

<u>Amy</u> a friend of mine started seeing this guy that had asked her out while they were working together, but she had returned to her home country when he made his intentions clear to her by phone, that he was serious. I'll call him <u>Raymond.</u>

Amy had recently recommitted her life to the Lord and was saving herself now for her husband to be. Raymond is a Christian man; they would often pray together and discuss the word of God during their phone conversations as they build their long distant relationship getting to know each other better as best they could.

As time passes about a year, Raymond asked Amy to come for a visit. He offered to pay for her plane ticket, she agreed to visit after much persuasion. Upon her second visit Raymond popped the big question and on one knee with engagement ring in hand he asked Amy to marry him, she said yes. Amy did not go back to her home country but stayed with her new fiancé as she now plans to get married.

Amy married Raymond and they started their journey as a Christian couple. They went to church together and lived a simple life but what Amy didn't know was that Raymond's family practiced witchcraft in their home country. She had only met his brother that lived with them. As years went by Amy began to notice abnormal behaviors in her husband and his brother, she said a strange thing would happen as soon as they were about to make love, she said "I would see the brother's face come up to her face in a quick vision, like a flash" but she didn't take it seriously. She didn't understand why that happens. She would be home alone all day until her husband comes, she had no money and was not working yet. The transition was hard from being independent, to becoming solely dependent on a man, all that was provided was her basic needs. Amy finally started working and her husband bought her a little car to start out with.

Raymond began to express that some of the things in the **<u>bible he did not agree with or believe.</u>** He would criticize her of her figure and express his disapproval very often as time goes by. They tried to have a child, but Amy had a miscarriage and had a hard time dealing with the loss. Along with his continuous rejection of her body. They went to marriage counseling once together; Amy went a few times after Raymond stopped going. He stopped being intimate with her completely and there was no affection. She would try to do things the way Raymond preferred, such as losing weight and how she spoke, but he wouldn't acknowledge her efforts.

He began to have hallucinations and became delusional. Amy had to rush him to the emergency room because he told her his heart was bleeding and there was something dripping blood on his head but there was no blood in sight among other things.

The doctors admitted him and gave him medications and transferred him to a Rehabilitation facility. Amy traveled back and forth from home to work to the facility with his clothes and necessities. There was a time when he didn't want to see anyone, only his brother could visit him.

Raymond got better and resumed normal life, he went back to work, and things began to feel normal again. But it didn't last long, he started having hallucinations again and one night he left the house for a walk, and he didn't return. Amy couldn't find him or reach him on his cell phone for one whole day and night, he was missing. She called the police and they put out a search for him with helicopters and the search team. They couldn't find him. Amy got a call from someone the next day at the hospital informing her that Raymond had checked himself in the hospital.

Raymond told the doctors that Amy is trying to kill him, and he doesn't want to see her. Amy burst out in tears. They assured her that they know he is not well. They kept him there, ran some test and gave him medication to calm him down but after a couple days they released him at his request because he came in on his own. Raymond went back home but things were never the same, he took his medication and tried to resume his life but at this time he was out of a job. Financially, Amy was struggling with all the bills, and they had recently bought a house together.

Raymond began to have episodes of hallucination again. That's when Amy found out he stopped taking his medication. They would argue about this, then he would take them, but he wasn't consistent and eventually they grew further apart.

Raymond asked her for a divorce which she began to file shortly after he requested it and as the filing was coming to an end, he told her he wanted to try again but Amy decided that she couldn't stay married to him anymore. **_They were not in agreement with anything at all_** and in addition to that, there was witchcraft interferences coming from his side of family. He was in constant contact with his family in his home country that are witchcraft practitioners.

Amy would notice a pattern that every time he spoke to them, he would have these episodes. He was warned by a deliverance minister that had prayed for him and through the power of the Holy Ghost he got delivered from heavy demonic oppression. He was told to cut all ties with them, but he didn't listen.

Ladies and men that are gentle. Please do not just marry a person because they have been going to church for years, do not marry a person because they have bible knowledge, do not marry a person because they pray with you. **Marry a person that has a <u>personal relationship</u> with Jesus Christ. Not a form of Godliness.**

Raymond and Amy where unequally yoked and were not ordained by God to be husband and wife. Raymond did not believe the whole bible and therefore did not live accordingly.

"16. Ye shall know them by <u>their fruits.</u> Do men gather grapes of thorns, or figs of thistles? 17. Even so every good tree bringeth forth good fruit; but a corrupt tree bringeth forth evil fruit. 18. A good tree cannot bring forth evil fruit, neither can a corrupt tree bring forth good fruit. 19. Every tree that bringeth not forth good fruit is hewn down and cast into the fire.20. Wherefore by their fruits ye shall know them". **Matthew 7:16 -20 KJV**

2 Corinthians 11:14 KJV *"And no marvel; for Satan himself is transformed into an angel of light".*

Matthew 7:15 KJV *"Beware of false prophets, which come to you in sheep's clothing, but inwardly they are ravening wolves."*

MAKE INFORMED DECISIONS

CHAPTER 14

Love Yourself

Genesis 2:7 *"And the Lord God formed man of the dust of the ground and <u>breathed into his nostrils the breath</u> of life; and* **man** *became <u>a living soul.</u>"*

Do you know how precious your soul is? You are a soul with a spirit that is encapsulated by your physical body. It is your soul that makes you different, unique and distinct from others. Your spirit is the life force in you. Who you are is the influence you have on others, the words that you speak, the thoughts that originates from your mind, your desires that springs from your core and the depth of your understanding.

When you get an ID card which is to identify who you are. This is the least of your identification, your height, weight, DOB, etc. But two things are always written on these ID cards. The date issued and the expiration date. Without these two an ID is invalid.

Does our soul expire? Do we need to <u>renew</u> our soul, because we have expired, being denied entry or access? When do we receive the identity of our soul? It's in the womb at our very conception. That's when we are issued our identity and it NEVER expires. What God has ordained you to be will never leave you. Even if you ignore it, treat it as nothing, forget it or worse never sought to know what your purpose was.

"Before <u>I formed thee in the belly,</u> I knew thee; and before thou camest forth out of the womb I sanctified thee, and I ordained thee a prophet unto the nations" Jeremiah 1:5 KJV

Before Jeremiah was conceived (formed in the belly) he had an identity, but he didn't receive it yet until conception. So was Isaac.

When you've accepted who God has created you to be, <u>then can you truly love yourself</u>. Many are still on this journey to find their true selves, traveling further away from the creator, seeking answers from His creation. Many have given up and accepted lies and calls it "their truth" but they are still NOT happy because they lack divine revelation.

In the scriptures you see where Paul wrote about the renewing of your mind.

Romans 12 :2KJV "And be not conformed to this world: but be ye **transformed by the renewing** of your mind, that ye may prove what is that good, and acceptable, and perfect, will of God."

<u>Definition from Merriam Webster.com</u>

Transform means – to change in composition or structure: to change the outward form or appearance of : to change in character or condition.

Renew means – to make like new: restore to freshness.

Transform your thinking **by** renewing your thoughts. You cannot stop thinking but you can <u>change</u> **how** you process the thoughts you think and choose what to think.

Philippians 4:8KJV

"Finally, brethren whatsoever things are true, whatsoever things are honest, whatsoever things are just, whatsoever things are pure, whatsoever things are lovely, whatsoever things are of good report; If there be any virtue, and if there be any praise, **<u>think</u>** on these things".

You have a WILL. This is the ability of your mind to choose among or between your desires.

This is displayed when you have to choose against your desire, to do what is right against what feels good. Because what <u>feels</u> good is not always right.

So, with the knowledge of what is actually good, your appetites, your vices, lust and rebellion is now pressed and bent, to **will** yourself towards righteousness, which goes against your fallen nature.

But as you renew your mind by thinking on these things mention in Philippians 4:8. The transformation will slowly be evident.

Can an Eagle that was adopted by a Hen, that only knew how to mother her chicks provide all the necessary training this baby eagle needs? This Mother Hen is treating this eagle like one of her own. Whose responsibility is it to go after their purpose? There will come a time when you have to leave the nest and pursue your identity, which will lead you to your destiny. The road map of your destiny was built in your identity.

<u>In order for you to love yourself, you must know who you are.</u>

I agree with Paul, that we should renew our minds, but I'll say as well, we are to discover ourselves!

Discover the original you that God predestined you to be before the fall of the first Adam. But now is made possible by the second Adam which is Jesus Christ.

Ephesians 1:3-5 KJV *"Blessed be the God and Father of our Lord Jesus Christ, who hath blessed us with all spiritual blessings in heavenly places in Christ....According as he hath chosen us in him <u>before the foundation of the world</u>, that we should be holy and without blame before him in love:*

<u>*Have predestinated*</u> *us unto the adoption of children by Jesus Christ to himself, according to the good pleasure of His will".*

Hebrews 2:6 KJV

*"But one in a certain place testified, saying, **what is man**, that thou art mindful of him? Or the son of man, that thou visitest him? Thou madest him a little lower than the angels; thou crownedst him with glory and honor, and didst set him over the works of thy hands."*

Genesis 2:7 KJV *" And the Lord God formed man of the dust of the ground, and breathed into his nostrils the breath of life; and man became a living soul ".*

We are living souls.

God, who is a Spirit, created (formed) us in His likeness and image, breathe into our nostrils His life (Spirit). That's what makes us so precious to Him, we are all a part of Him. His Spirit made our soul come alive to be a "**living – soul**", this is a manifestation of God's existence, in every human being.

I didn't know how to love myself for a long time. I never heard about loving yourself until I was an adult in my early 30's, and when I thought about it, I didn't know where to start.

All I knew was to show love, respect and kindness to others, by what I was told to do, but how do I show myself that I love me? And did I love myself, to show myself love in the first place? I went to the mirror and looked at myself and I was sad.

I was so upset with myself, angry, disappointed and hurt. I did not like looking in the mirror. I remembered a time in my life where I had started to avoid mirrors. I would use it just for combing my hair, not even for dressing. For approximately 4 years I didn't take pictures.

My poor decisions were my identity, and its consequences was the life I knew. I was living a consequential life, in the permissive will of God.

My living soul was sick. It needed healing, it needed power, it needed the breath of God to breathe life into it again. As I was thinking of how this healing was going to take place, this thought immediately came to me, the word of God, read His word came to my mind.

John 6:63KJV *"It is the spirit that quickeneth; the flesh profiteth nothing: the words that I speak unto you, they are **spirit**, and they are **life**".*

These are the words of Jesus Christ, to some this may seem like foolishness but to many of us without the word of God, we would be rotting in our graves or in a mental institution. When you read the word of God, your soul begins to receive new life

Romans 10:17 *"So then faith cometh by hearing, and hearing by the word of God".* Hearing the word of God is like giving your soul a jump start, it revives you. Your spirit gets a renewal.

Have you ever wondered why wealthy people commit suicide, why they're constantly depressed and full of anxiety, some die from overdose, because they have no peace within, no peace in their souls?

What about the Pastors that commit suicide you might ask? Shouldn't they know better? Oh yes.

But even Pastors suffer in silence under pressure of being there for everyone but has no one to turn to but God, and in a moment of weakness, not being sober minded, because some Pastors think they cannot show weakness, they get weary in well doing and they faint. They start doubting and giving up, in that split second of decision they give in to the lies of satan and his words, which are words of death.

Absolutely no one is exempt from temptation, we are going to be tempted, tested and tried all the days of our lives. Every single one of us has our weak and weakest moments. That is why we must be strong IN the Lord.

Philippians 4:13 "I can do all things through Christ that strengthens me".

When your strength is gone then the joy of the Lord is your strength. Why worry yourself to death when you know God is in control, take control of your mind using the word of God.

His word says ask and it shall be given………seek and you shall find. Ask by faith, seek by faith. When you've come to the end of your rope and you feel like throwing in the towel, you must ask for HELP. I did.

Exodus 17:11 -13KJV

"And it came to pass, when Moses held up his hand, that Israel prevailed: and when he let down his hand, Amalek prevailed.

*12.<u>But Moses hands were heavy</u>; and they took a stone, and put it under him, and he sat thereon and **Aaron and Hur stayed up his hands**, the one on the one side and the other on the other side; and his hands were steady until the going down of the sun.*

13. And Joshua discomfited Amalek and his people with the edge of the sword".

The strongest of us need help at times. We need others to help us get through life's challenges. There are times God will give a person a word of encouragement in a moment of despair to revive your faith and hope, but if you isolate yourself how can they reach you? Yes, God can send manna from heaven, or you might get visited by an angel to rescue you out of danger in a split second, but God uses His servants here on earth to minister to his children and sometimes a complete stranger. Let God use his genuine servants to help you in a time of need.

When you turn away <u>genuine</u> help you turn away the hand of God.

Give the stress to GOD! And let Him do what only He can.

You might be reading and saying to yourself, it's easier said than done but let me ask you this, do you really trust God? Do you? then prove it.

When you love yourself, you will take care of yourself, and who better to take good care of you than who created you.

1Peter 5:7 *"Casting all your care upon him; for He careth for you"*

Trust Him to take care of you.

Love yourself by being kind to you and to others, by taking time to count the cost of every decision you are making, by preparing yourself to reap the harvest of what you've sown, by being responsible and accountable for your actions, by forgiving yourself, by taking some me time, by deciding to stop when you have had enough, by moving on to what will fulfill your destiny and … *"forgetting those things which are behind"* **Philippians 3:13KJV**…by starting over a fresh, by taking a moment to acknowledge your weaknesses and your strengths. Once you have identified and confessed your weaknesses, God will give you the strength and the resources to overcome, with that strength you are now able to help those that are weak.

Love yourself by giving yourself to God your heavenly Father, accept His LOVE through His Son Jesus Christ. God's love will never fail or give up.

You are created by Love, you are loved! LOVE loves you!

GIVE YOURSELF A CHANCE TO BE LOVED BY YOU.

CHAPTER 15

Start over strong

After the chaos, relax! breathe and find a place to be quiet. Gather yourself and be one with yourself. Knowing that God has kept you through it and he is going to keep doing just that. Live in the moment of complete freedom. Live in an attitude of gratitude, enjoying the little things and simple pleasures, like having some ice-cream, an early morning run and enjoy the scent of fresh flowers.

You are alive to live. Live again and live again STRONG!

When you start over strong, you are strengthened by your weakness. It's because you overcame it, you now have the strength to fight your way through.

Begin to set goals for personal development. Make a list and set time of accomplishment. Make time for giving back too.

Be proactive, plan ahead and see yourself at least 2years into the future and work towards that image. A lot of us plan, but we don't do anything we planned to do. The plan stays on the paper or in our heads and we forget it because of all the other things that demands our attention.

We are moving from one stage of our lives into the next and that takes action.

Live the life you really were meant to live.

Many of us live in denial, thinking we have to accept the life that we happen to be living. There are situations that occurred without our control, and you may feel like a hostage to your circumstances. I understand that, but you don't have to be a hostage. Situations do not dictate our lives. Who or what are you living for?

Life is all about starting over, look at the seasons. Winter has his job, so does spring, summer and fall and the cycle starts over again and again. Every day we wake up, get dressed, go to work, go back home, go to bed, sleep and do the same thing the next day and every day. The next generation produces the next and so on and so on......

The difference is you are a human being given one life to live only once with many opportunities, some you will have to create, but what matters most is making the right choices with each day you start over. Fulfilling your purpose in each day with the right spouse and individuals God has assigned to you on your journey to help you fulfill your God given destiny.

Am I the reason this keeps happening? You may ask yourself this question. It's so easy to blame others for hurting us, pointing the finger away from you and not to you.

There comes a time in our lives when we must look at ourselves and admit what we did wrong. It's not all the other person's fault. We made the decision, we walked, drove, or took the plane there, we signed the contract and agreed. Why did we do it? The answers are many.

You must stop the blame game and start looking for the repeated mistakes you've somehow overlooked. Is there a pattern in your choices? Are your choices giving you the same results? You've changed location, your job, your circle of friends, but the same thing keeps happening. Little or no business, no promotion or your laid off, so called friends turns out to be back and front stabbers.

Ask yourself the question, is it me?

Choices

We must make better choices! How can we do this? By changing our mindset.

Break the pattern by breaking the habits, choose to do things differently.

Sometimes we get comfortable in the pattern, because of fear of failure, but the sad thing is, by staying in a state of fear, is accepting failure and embracing the brainwash, that playing it safe is best or staying in the position until better comes, this is actually dangerous and not true.

Everything that's rewarding takes hard work, sacrifice and some kind of risk.

<u>Make a decision that will bring change and improve your life</u>.

Look in the mirror and ask yourself what am I doing that is hurting me? We can't lie to ourselves, and we must face the truth in order to stop making the same wrong moves.

Our weaknesses are working against us, so we must give them to the one who will strengthen us.

"Finally, my brethren, be strong in the Lord and in the power of his might."
Ephesians 6:10

Only the strength of the Lord can empower us to overcome weaknesses and dysfunctional habits that will eventually terminate destinies if we don't acknowledge and address them.

If you don't make up your mind, to will yourself, to decide against your addiction, being stubborn, hateful and negative. The cycle will continue and the results will always be wasteful and destructive. Some people are addicted to shopping and their finances are nowhere, they will shop until there is not a dollar left in their name.

Then you have those with an attitude problem that will take them straight to prison. Have you ever met a person that keeps getting lock up? What are they doing that keeps placing them in the same place for correction? The person correcting them are tired of them.

It all starts in the MIND, your mind might need deliverance from an invisible evil influence, or you simply need to **change your mind** by deciding to do so. Our decisions determine what move we are going to make next. May God order the steps you take next. Let's start over with better choices.

You have the power to change your mind.
To change your circumstance.
To change the outcome.
To change how you think.

LET GOD'S CHOICE BE YOURS.

www.ingramcontent.com/pod-product-compliance
Lightning Source LLC
Chambersburg PA
CBHW071505070526
44578CB00001B/453